Tropical Drinks

and

Gelatin Party Shots

HAWAI'I'S
Tropical
Drinks
and
Gelatin
Party
Shots

Mark Sullivan

photography by
Ray Wong

Library of Congress Cataloging-in-Publication Data

Sullivan, Mark (Mark J.), 1962-
  Hawaii's tropical drinks and gelatin party shots / Mark Sullivan.
      p. cm.
  Summary: "A collection of tropical drink and gelatin shot recipes"--Provided by publisher.
  Includes index.
  ISBN 1-56647-777-8 (hardcover : alk. paper)
  1. Cocktails--Hawaii. I. Title.
  TX951.S945 2006
  641.8'7409969--dc22

                    2006007364

First Printing, May 2006
1 2 3 4 5 6 7 8 9

ISBN-10: 1-56647-777-8
ISBN-13: 978-1-56647-777-2

Design by Mardee Domingo Melton

Mutual Publishing, LLC
1215 Center Street, Suite 210
Honolulu, Hawai'i 96816
Ph: (808) 732-1709
Fax: (808) 734-4094
email: mutual@mutualpublishing.com
www.mutualpublishing.com

Printed in Korea

Dedicated to:

My late, great big brother

Mike "Sully" Sullivan

November 4, 1955–June 15, 2003

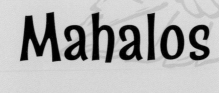

Mahalos

First of all, a big mahalo to everyone who
was an inspiration for any of these cocktails
and to all my friends and coworkers who
acted (knowingly or not) as my guinea pigs.
You all know who you are.

To Dean Coffin and Al LaBernz, wherever you
are, for teaching me the skills way back when.

To my old friend Dave McAteer for the advice
and years of comic relief.

To Steve and Gaylene Phillips for the advice
and moral support.

Most importantly, to my wife Leila for putting
up with this craziness for all these years.

Table of Contents

Introduction

My first bartending job was in a seafood restaurant in Vermont back in 1986. It started out as something to do while I applied to medical school, became something I did for cash during medical school, and ended up as a career after I dropped out of medical school. That life just wasn't for me; I loved the work but hated the business. After a few months of bartending in a pub in my hometown, I moved to the Big Island for a change of scenery, a fresh start, and an escape from the harsh below-zero winters of the Northeast. I used to say I became a member of "Club Ex-Med." I tended bar at a resort hotel for a couple of years, and later at a restaurant/nightclub in Waikoloa. I moved to O'ahu in 1994 with my then-girlfriend (and now wife) so she could finish up her undergrad work and attend law school at UH Mānoa, and I bartended at an ocean-front dining establishment in downtown Honolulu for over ten years. Along the way I met lots of people, had lots of fun, and really fell in love with all that is Hawai'i—not only with its beauty but with its culture, people, and way of life. I'm proud to call Hawai'i my home.

Now, tending bar in Hawai'i is really just like tending bar anywhere else—except for the fact that you live and work in paradise—but work is still work. Doing any job long enough can get monotonous at times. I can't even begin to count the thousands of Mai Tai's, Chi Chi's, and Lava Flows I've made over the years. Trust me, making a hundred of the same things every night can get to you after a while. Purely for my own amusement, I started experimenting with different combinations of liquors, liqueurs, and mixers, looking for some fresh cocktail ideas to add to my repertoire. The latest trend in the liquor industry has been the creation of fruit-flavored vodkas and rums, and most of them seemed to go well with all the fresh fruit and juices I had at my disposal. Every time a distributor introduced a new product I was like a kid with a new toy, tasting it in every combination I could think of.

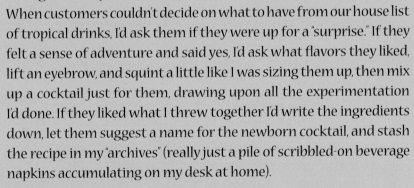

At first the hard part was finding a "guinea pig" to test my new recipes out on, but that got easier as time went on. Friends and coworkers were always willing, but I needed to get random strangers to try the new stuff too. When customers couldn't decide on what to have from our house list of tropical drinks, I'd ask them if they were up for a "surprise." If they felt a sense of adventure and said yes, I'd ask what flavors they liked, lift an eyebrow, and squint a little like I was sizing them up, then mix up a cocktail just for them, drawing upon all the experimentation I'd done. If they liked what I threw together I'd write the ingredients down, let them suggest a name for the newborn cocktail, and stash the recipe in my "archives" (really just a pile of scribbled-on beverage napkins accumulating on my desk at home).

Some of my concoctions made it onto our house drink menu and became pretty popular, and there were even a few regulars who would have one of the drinks I'd created for them on almost every visit. After a while, shaking and blending tropical drinks, even with all the fresh fruit and juices I had available, began to seem a little mundane. Just about every bartender has come up with a few of their own recipes for those types of drinks. I wanted to do something unique, so my quest for new cocktail ideas took me to the gelatin aisles of local grocery stores. Thus began my interest in (some would say sick obsession with) making gelatin shot cocktails.

Gelatin shots are a great way to add something different to any party. They're really easy to make and everybody loves them at birthday parties, barbecues, wherever. I find that they're especially

good for tailgate parties at sporting events because you can make them well in advance, they don't require any equipment after they're made, and they're easy to take along. I just put them in zip lock bags and pack them in a cooler with plenty of ice. My gelatin shot making has become pretty exotic over the years, just mixing plain old vodka with random flavors of gelatin seemed a little too ordinary to be served at parties attended by a bunch of bartenders. Many of these recipes are classic cocktails that I've adapted for gelatin, and I've also come up with quite a few of my own.

All this experimentation with gelatin came about when I started making them for an annual tailgate party my wife and I throw at the Pro Bowl NFL All-Star Game, played each year at Aloha Stadium here on O'ahu. Now, tailgate parties are a huge part of attending every football game, both college and professional, just about everywhere. I think it's the annual Florida Gators/Georgia Bulldogs game that's infamously referred to as "The World's Largest Outdoor Cocktail Party." I get my hands on more and more tickets each year—for the last few I've had a block of 30 seats—and get a bunch of friends together to spend the day eating, drinking, and watching NFL football. It's always been a big event around here, partly because it's the only professional sports event that people in Hawai'i get to attend live, but mostly because it's the last NFL game of the season, time for one last bash until next year. It's really just one big party, and the fact that the players are in Hawai'i after their season's over to take a little vacation and never really play all that hard adds to the festive atmosphere. The parking lot is filled with smoking barbecue grills, loud music (there's usually a live band or two), and lots and lots of beer.

After a few years, we got tired of having beer as the only adult beverage available. I remembered having a great time at a barbecue a few years back where someone had made a bunch of gelatin shots, so I decided to experiment with a few gelatin cocktail ideas I had. That year, I made up a batch of 75 gelatin shooters for the tailgate, little did I know they'd be gone in a matter of minutes and everyone would want more. Fine, so the next year I doubled the number to 150 shooters and, again, all were gone very quickly. If there's one thing I can't stand it's running out of liquor at a party, so the following year I made 300 shooters of assorted flavors. Once again, all gone before game time. (Okay, so I hang out with a bunch of winos.) The next year, on a dare I made 600 gelatin shooters, and felt the need to come up with even more recipes. Mai Tais, Razztinis Long Island Iced Teas, and, my personal favorite, the Surfer on Acid. So many that I had to start making them more than a week in advance and find a friend with room in his refrigerator to help store them all before game day. This time there were plenty to go around, enough to share with neighboring tailgaters, and even a few to take on the walk from the parking lot to the stadium.

Our having so many of those things ensures that everyone has a great time. We've come up with a few drinking games that are always good for a few laughs. Doing an "aerial" is tossing a wad of gelatin in the air and trying to catch it in your mouth. Toss it too high and miss and you'll get a face full or wear it on your shirt. The main thing to remember about gelatin shots is that, even though they taste like candy, they're pretty potent. Each shooter is half alcohol and they can sneak up on you if you're not careful. Every year someone has a few too many and does something comical. It gets a little crazy, but all in all, everyone has a great time and stays safe.

Since then, the Pro Bowl tailgate parties we throw have become a legendary event. I have a few friends I see only about once a year, usually around the end of January, asking where and when that year's tailgater will be and how many gelatin shooters I'll be making. When friends and relatives fly out from the mainland for a visit, they usually plan their trips around the Pro Bowl. It's really all because of the gelatin shooters. If you ever go to the game, try to find us in the parking lot. Just look for a bunch of drunks slurping gelatin out of little plastic cups. Remember, there's always room for gelatin.

The idea for this book came to me when somebody, after eyeing all the gelatin shooters I've made and sucked down a few, said: "You really should write a book." I kind of laughed it off but realized that the gelatin shots and other assorted cocktails I'd created generally went over well and I'd accumulated quite a pile of recipes in "the archives" so, why not? Okay, here it all is. You asked for it. Everything you need to know about how to make gelatin shot cocktails like a pro, plus some funky cocktail recipes from my archives. Enjoy yourselves. Remember, always use alcohol responsibly, never drink and drive, tip your servers and bartenders, and, above all, be good.

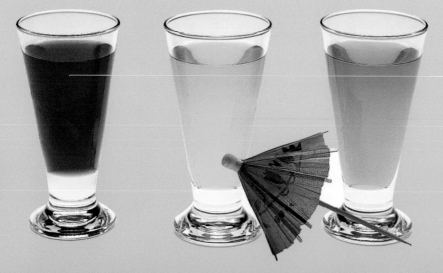

Cocktail Mixing
Tips FOR THE HOME BARTENDER

Every cocktail needs a little mixing in one way or another. Liquors and juices have different viscosities so just pouring the ingredients in a glass won't do. Tropical cocktails with multiple ingredients should always get a thorough mixing to ensure a nice, smooth drink with all the flavors in every sip.

SHAKING

There are many different types of cocktail shakers and strainers, all work pretty well, and all are usually easy to find at any kitchen supply store. There are two basic designs: the Boston-style shaker glass and tin combo (which most professional bartenders prefer) and the type with a lid and built-in strainer. Either type works just fine for shaking cocktails at home.

Shaking a cocktail on the rocks is the best way to get a thorough mixing of all the ingredients. One of the biggest and most common mistakes that bartenders make is shaking a drink too much. Shaking too hard or for too long will break up all the ice and result in a watery, diluted cocktail. When James Bond orders a martini "shaken, not stirred," he's really saying he prefers his vodka watered-down, weak, and wimpy. One or two good shakes is usually plenty, even pouring the drink back and forth into another glass will do if you don't have a shaker handy. The only time a cocktail should be shaken good and hard is if the recipe calls for a squeeze of lemon or lime. For those drinks, a good hard shaking breaks up the fruit, knocking the pulp into the mixture, which adds more citrus flavor and smoothness to the concoction.

BLENDING

Mixing up a cocktail with ice in a blender will make a nice, frosty drink, always very refreshing on a sunny afternoon, but blending up all that ice will add water to the mixture. I usually put all the ingredients into the blender cup first, then gradually add just enough ice to thicken the drink and make it cold. Too much ice will result in a drink that's too thick and diluted. Also, make sure to run the blender long enough to break up all the ice, making the cocktail nice and smooth.

Frozen drinks with fresh fruit are great, but if you're going to make a lot of them for a party it's helpful to purée the fruit beforehand with a little concentrated sweet and sour (frozen concentrated lemonade works well too) in a ratio of about five parts fruit to one part sour. This will add some body and tartness to the purée, resulting in a thicker mixture that won't be diluted too much by the ice in the blender. Another way to create a good fruit mix for the blender (and the method I prefer) is to use frozen concentrated fruit juice in place of fresh fruit. Just use the concentrate right out of the can. This allows for the extra water that comes along with blending the mix with ice. For drinks with ice cream in the recipe, you'll only need a very small amount of ice (just two or three cubes) to thicken and chill the mixture.

BASIC BAR TOOLS

There are a few basic bar tools that are a must for any home bartender. All are available at most restaurant or kitchen supply stores.

Cocktail Shaker—Pictured is the "Boston" style shaker preferred by most professional bartenders. It consists of a mixing glass and stainless steel shaker tin. Another type available is the "Standard" shaker, one with a lid and built-in strainer.

Strainer—Also known as a Hawthorn strainer, it fits on the top of a shaker tin or mixing glass for straining a cocktail from the ice.

Bar Spoon—Long handled for stirring a cocktail in any size glass.

Waiter's Corkscrew—A handy tool for removing wine corks, it also has a small knife blade and bottle opener.

Jigger—For measuring cocktail ingredients, the best are stainless steel, double ended, and come in a variety of sizes.

Muddler—Shaped like a small baseball bat, handy for crushing cocktail ingredients like fruit, mint, etc.

Can and Bottle Opener—'nuf said.

Pour Spouts—Made from metal or plastic, they come in all sorts of sizes, and make pouring from a liquor bottle easier with less probability of making a mess.

Glassware
Basics

There are many different shapes and styles of glassware, each having a few characteristics that make them handy for serving specific kinds of cocktails. Since I suggest a glass with each of the recipes, let's go over the basics. All of these types come in a wide range of sizes and are pretty easy to find at any kitchen or restaurant supply store.

Shot Glass
2 to 4 ounces is probably the most common size, the best for layering liquors, and can also be used for measuring.

Rocks or Old-fashioned
7 or so ounces with a heavy base and tapered to a wider lip, used mostly for liquors without mixers on ice or for larger volume shooters.

Pint or Double Old-fashioned
14 to 16 ounces, a larger version of the rocks glass. A multipurpose glass for beer, tropicals, and frozen drinks.

Martini
6 to 8 ounces, classic stemmed V-shape, best for chilled liquors, shooters, and other sipping drinks.

Champagne Flute
6 to 8 ounces, tall and thin with a stem and heavy base. Really designed for sipping bubbly, but I find them handy for shooters as well.

Hurricane
14 to 16 ounces, a general category of big, curvy, exotic looking glassware best for exotic drinks like tropicals and frozen drinks.

Tropical Cocktails

Most of these recipes will require a 14-ounce or larger glass of any type. These are exotic drinks so the more exotic the glass, like a curvy hurricane-style glass, the better the presentation. All should be served on the rocks.

Koko's Melon Adventure

Traditional Hawaiian Mai Tai

Lehua

No Fear

The Big E

Mackin' Mai Tai

Big Daddy

Diamond Head

Pineapple Breeze

Big Island Iced Tea

Pai'ea Punch

Natasha

Pupule Punch

Wendella

Kat Skratch

Rough Sex

Brainless

Electric Cobra

Gimme A Minute

Mountain Doo Kine

Blue Surf

Koko's
Melon Adventure

This was the first drink I ever came up with after being asked to make something new for a customer, in this case an old friend of mine. It was kind of an adventure as I had no idea what I was doing or if it would taste any good. Luckily, it turned out great, slightly sweet, and very refreshing.

1-1/2 ounces Stolchnaya Vodka
3/4 ounce Midori Melon Liqueur
Splash sweetened lime juice
1 ounce Pineapple Juice
1 ounce Sprite
2 ounces Sweet and Sour

Shake and serve in a tall 14-ounce Hurricane glass, garnish with a slice of fresh lime and sprig of mint.

Koko's
Melon Adventure

Traditional
Hawaiian Mai Tai

I'm including this recipe because so many places screw it up. If I order one and it shows up pink-colored or with OJ in it, I send it back.

1-1/2 ounces Light Rum
1/3 ounce Orange Curacao
1/3 ounce Orgeat Syrup
1-1/2 ounces Pineapple Juice
1-1/2 ounces Sweet and Sour

Shake. Float 1-1/2 ounces Dark Rum, the darker the better. Serve in a 14-ounce double old-fashioned glass and garnish with a fresh pineapple spear, bamboo orchid, and a parasol.

Lehua

A friend of mine asked for something strong but refreshing. With lots of different juices, it takes a while to make when the bar is busy, so of course, she'd always bring a bunch of her friends in to drink them, all night long.

2 ounces Absolut Citron Vodka
1 ounce Sweet and Sour
1 ounce Pineapple Juice
1 ounce Sprite
1 ounce Orange Juice
1 ounce Cranberry Juice

Shake and serve in a tall pint or double old-fashioned glass, garnish with a fresh slice of orange and sprig of mint.

No Fear

1-1/2 ounces Hana Bay 151 Rum
1/2 ounce Peach Schnapps
1/2 ounce DeKuyper Tropical Pineapple
2 ounces Liliko'i (passion fruit) Juice
2 ounces Sprite

Shake. Float 1/2 ounce Blue Curacao.
Serve in a 14-ounce Hurricane glass,
garnish with a fresh lime wheel
and bamboo orchid.

The Big E

The Big E

1 ounce 151 Proof Rum
1/2 ounce Midori Melon Liqueur
1/2 ounce Grand Marnier
1/2 ounce Dark Rum
1 ounce Pineapple Juice
1 ounce Sprite
2 ounces Cranberry Juice

Shake and serve in a frozen, cored-out pineapple, garnish with a fresh bamboo orchid and a parasol.

Not to be left out, Koko's husband Erik asked for his own cocktail, a big, potent drink for a big guy. We almost called this one the "Elephant Gun."

Mackin' Mai Tai

A favorite of my old pal Angus Crock.

1-1/2 ounces Mt. Gay Eclipse Rum
1/2 ounce Orange Curacao
1/4 ounce Grenadine
2 ounces Orange Juice
2 ounces Pineapple Juice

Shake. Float 1-1/2 ounces Myers's Dark Rum. Serve in a tall 14-ounce Hurricane glass, garnish with a fresh orange slice and a maraschino cherry.

Big Daddy

Years ago I worked with a server named Samara— a pretty name for a pretty girl. Anyway, she wrongly accused me of never getting her name right, so for a few laughs I called her anything but Samara. She asked one day if I had a nickname I liked and I said "Please, call me Big Daddy." She proceeded to only call me "Big Daddy" thereafter. It was pretty funny, so I never told her I was only kidding.

2 ounces Myers's Dark Rum
4 ounces Cranberry Juice
Squeeze of one lemon wedge

Shake and serve in a tall pint glass, garnish with a fresh slice of lemon.

Diamond Head

1 ounce Hana Bay 151 Rum
1/2 ounce Hana Bay Dark Rum
1/2 ounce Kahlua
2 ounces Pineapple Juice
2 ounces Sprite

Shake and serve in a 14-ounce Hurricane glass and garnish with a pineapple slice, mint sprig, and a parasol.

Pineapple Breeze

1-1/2 ounces Malibu Pineapple Rum
3/4 ounce Kahana Royale Macadamia Nut Liqueur
2 ounces Pineapple Juice
2 ounces Sweet and Sour

Shake and serve in a 14-ounce Hurricane glass, garnish with a pineapple slice and mint sprig.

Big Island Iced Tea

1/2 ounce Vodka
1/2 ounce Gin
1/2 ounce Light Rum
1/2 ounce DeKuyper Tropical Pineapple
1 ounce Sweet and Sour
3 ounces Coke
Squeeze of one lemon wedge

Shake and serve in a tall pint glass and garnish with a lemon slice, mint sprig, and sugarcane stick.

Big Island
Iced Tea

Pai'ea
Punch

Pai'ea Punch

For B and Deano…

1 ounce Myers's Dark Rum
1-1/2 ounces DeKuyper Tropical Pineapple
2 ounces Cranberry Juice
2 ounces Sprite

Shake and serve in a tall pint glass, garnish with a lemon wheel and orchid.

Natasha

3/4 ounce Peach Schnapps
3/4 ounce DeKuyper Sour Apple Pucker
3/4 ounce 151 Proof Rum
2 ounces Cranberry Juice
1 ounce Sweet and Sour
Squeeze of one lemon wedge

Shake and serve in a 14-ounce Hurricane glass, garnish with a slice of granny smith apple and sprig of mint.

Pupule Punch

3/4 ounce DeKuyper Tropical Pineapple
3/4 ounce DeKuyper Sour Apple Pucker
3/4 ounce Myers's Dark Rum
2 ounces Liliko'i (passion fruit) Juice
2 ounces Cranberry Juice

Shake and serve in a 14-ounce Hurricane glass, garnish with a pineapple slice and parasol.

Wendella

1 ounce Hana Bay 151 Rum
3/4 ounce DeKuyper Tropical Pineapple
1 ounce Mango Purée
2 ounces Cranberry Juice
1 ounce Sprite

Shake and serve in a 14-ounce Hurricane glass, garnish with a fresh slice of mango, mint sprig, and parasol.

Kat
Skratch

1 ounce Kahlua
1 ounce Stoly Vanilla
1 ounce Orange Juice
1 ounce Pineapple Juice
1 ounce Ginger Ale

Shake and serve in a 14-ounce Hurricane glass, garnish with three fresh coffee beans, pineapple spear, and parasol.

Rough Sex

1 ounce Hana Bay 151 Rum
1 ounce Peach Schnapps
3 ounces Cranberry Juice
1 ounce Orange Juice

Shake and serve in a 14-ounce Hurricane glass, garnish with a fresh lime wheel and maraschino cherry.

Brainless

1 ounce Kuya Fusion Rum
1 ounce Tuaca
1 ounce Pineapple Juice
1 ounce Sweet and Sour
2 ounces Ginger Ale

Shake and serve in a double old-fashioned glass, garnish with a pineapple slice and bamboo orchid.

Electric
Cobra

Electric
Cobra

1 ounce Bacardi Razz Rum
1/2 ounce Southern Comfort
1/2 ounce Hana Bay 151 Rum
2 ounces Sweet and Sour
2 ounces Sprite
1/2 ounce Blue Curacao

Shake and serve in a 14-ounce Hurricane glass, garnish with a lemon wheel, bamboo orchid, and a blue parasol.

One of my regulars came up with the name and then asked for a cocktail to go with it.

Gimme
a Minute

1 ounce Blue Wave Raspberry Vodka
1 ounce DeKuyper Sour Apple Pucker
3 ounces Sprite
Squeeze of one lemon wedge

*Shake and serve in a 14-ounce double old-fashioned
glass, garnish with a slice of granny smith apple and
a blue parasol.*

Mountain Doo Kine

"Da Kine" is easily the most over used phrase in Hawaiian Pidgin language, for when you can't remember the name of something. Now, "Doo Kine" is a phrase used in place of something dirty or otherwise unmentionable. Anyway, this drink is an "Adults Only" version of a popular soft drink... that Willie Boy and I came up with.

1-1/2 ounces Absolut Mandarin
1/2 ounce Midori Melon Liqueur
1/2 ounce Lemonade Concentrate
1 ounce Orange Juice
2 ounces Miller Lite Beer

Shake and serve in a tall pint glass, garnish with fresh slices of lime, lemon, orange, and a maraschino cherry.

Tropical Cocktails

27

Blue
Surf

1 ounce Kuya Fusion Rum
1 ounce DeKuyper Island Blue Pucker
1/2 ounce Blue Curacao
3 ounces Sprite
Squeeze of one lemon wedge

Shake and serve in a 14-ounce Hurricane glass, garnish with a lemon wheel, two maraschino cherries, and a blue parasol.

Blue Surf

Bloody Mary
Mix

1-1/2 ounces Vodka
3/4 ounce Bloody Mary mix
  (see note)
4 ounces Tomato Juice (or V8)

Shake and serve on the rocks in a pint glass rimmed with celery salt and garnish with a stalk of fresh celery.

Note: I usually make this up in advance and keep it in a plastic squeeze bottle in the fridge. It should stay fresh, refrigerated, for a week or so.

I became a connoisseur of the Bloody Mary long ago, making them by the dozen while watching football games with a few friends. Customers of mine have asked for this recipe for years, and I told them to wait and just buy the book.

The recipe below makes enough mix for about 20 drinks.

4 heaping tsp. prepared Horseradish
4 ounces Worcestershire Sauce
4 tsp. celery salt
2 tsp. crushed Black Pepper
2 tsp. Tabasco Sauce
Juice from one whole lemon

Here are a few suggestions to change the spices a little:
Add just a pinch of basil
Substitute 2 ounces dill pickle juice for the lemon juice
For a little Asian flair, substitute 2 tsp. Wasabi Paste for the horseradish.

Shooters

These shooter recipes should make a 5- or 6-ounce cocktail. For all of these recipes, place the ingredients in a shaker glass with ice and shake as directed. Straining each drink into a well-chilled glass insures the concoction will stay fresh and cold with every sip.

Kohala Lighthouse
Phone Call to God
Aloha 737
Jelly Donut
Kickin' Chicken
Hawaiian Delight
Maaary
Tootsie Pop
B-2 Stealth
Waimānalo
Carnival Ride
Milf
Red Hot Nuggets
Molten Martini

Irish Crackhead
Angry Juice
Fruit Loop
U-Boat
Hey Renee
Whisky Adobo
Dirty Sanchez
Okinawan Pineapple
Jagertini
Bunda Lani
Z Tini
Shoot Z Root
Green Geisha

Kohala
Lighthouse

Kohala
Lighthouse

1-1/2 ounces Stolichnaya Vodka
1/2 ounce Grand Marnier
Splash Rose's Lime Juice
Squeeze four lime wedges

Shake well and strain into a chilled champagne flute, garnish with a lime wheel.

Phone Call to God

1/2 ounce Vodka
1/2 ounce Gin
1/2 ounce Rum
1/2 ounce Triple Sec
1/2 ounce Tequila
1 ounce Orange Juice
Splash Grenadine

I pinched this recipe from Dougie, a former colleague of mine back East, who admitted he'd also pinched the recipe from a friend of his.

Shake and strain into a chilled 7-ounce rocks or old-fashioned glass.

Aloha 737

1/2 ounce Keoki Kona Coffee Liqueur
1/2 ounce E&J Brandy Cream
1/2 ounce Kahana Royale Macadamia Nut Liqueur

Layer the ingredients in the order listed into a shot glass.

Jelly
Donut

1 ounce Absolut Raspberry Vodka
1 ounce Chambord
1 ounce Half and Half

Shake once and strain into sugar-rimmed martini glass.

Kickin'
Chicken

1 ounce Wild Turkey 101 Proof
1 ounce Amaretto

Shake and strain into a 3-ounce shot or 7-ounce old-fashioned glass.

Hawaiian Delight

1-1/2 ounce Bacardi Limon Rum
1 ounce Peach Schnapps
1 ounce Liliko'i (passion fruit) Juice

*Shake once and strain into a chilled
7-ounce chilled old-fashioned glass.*

Maaary

1 ounce Stoly Strawberry
1 ounce DeKuyper Sour Apple Pucker
1 ounce Cranberry Juice
Squeeze three lime wedges

*Shake well and strain into a chilled 7-ounce martini
glass, garnish with a fresh lime wheel.*

Tootsie Pop

1 ounce Absolut Citron
1/2 ounce Kahlua
1 ounce Sprite

Shake once and strain into a chilled 7-ounce martini glass, garnish with a lemon wheel.

B-2 Stealth

This one sneaks right up to you and drops a bomb.

1 ounce 151 Proof Rum
1 ounce Peach Schnapps
1 ounce Pineapple Juice

Shake once and strain into a chilled 7-ounce old-fashioned glass.

Waimānalo
Carnival
Ride

Deano had plans to take his three very young daughters to the Waimānalo Carnival in the morning, and wanted one drink before heading home. He said: "This is my carnival ride."

1 ounce Absolut Mandarin
1/2 ounce Absolut Raspberry
1/2 ounce DeKuyper Sour Apple Pucker
1/2 ounce Cranberry Juice
1/2 ounce Sweet and Sour

Shake once and strain into a chilled 7-ounce martini glass, garnish with fresh lime and orange slices and a bamboo orchid.

Waimānalo
Carnival Ride

Milf

3/4 ounce Hana Bay 151 Rum
3/4 ounce Peach Schnapps
3/4 ounce DeKuyper Tropical Pineapple
1/2 ounce Cranberry Juice
1/2 ounce Pineapple Juice
1/2 ounce Ginger Ale

Shake once and strain into a chilled 7-ounce martini glass, garnish with a fresh pineapple slice, bamboo orchid, and pink parasol.

Red Hot Nuggets

Layer in a shot glass:
1/2 ounce Amaretto
1/2 ounce Frangelico
1/2 ounce Hana Bay 151 Rum
1/2 pint beer

Light the 151 on fire, drop into beer glass, and chug.

Molten
Martini

1 ounce Malibu Pineapple Rum
1 ounce DeKuyper Tropical Pineapple
1 ounce Cranberry Juice
Squeeze three lime wedges

*Shake well and strain into a chilled 7-ounce
martini glass, garnish with a fresh lime wheel.*

Irish
Crackhead

1 ounce Bailey's Irish Cream
1 ounce 99 Bananas
1 ounce 151 Proof Rum

*Shake and strain into a chilled 7-ounce
martini glass, garnish with a slice
of banana and a dollop of whipped cream.*

Angry Juice

Something my sister Diane and I came up with while having a few at Red Square in Burlington, Vermount.

"Like a Red Bull in a China Shop"

1 ounce José cuervo Gold Tequila
1 ounce Midori Melon Liqueur
2 ounces Red Bull energy drink

Shake once and strain into a chilled 7-ounce old-fashioned glass, garnish with a fresh lime wheel.

Shooters

44

Fruit Loop

1/2 ounce Mt. Gay Eclipse Rum
1/2 ounce Midori Melon Liqueur
1/2 ounce Peach Schnapps
1/2 ounce Orange Juice
1/2 ounce Pineapple Juice
1/2 ounce Cranberry Juice

Shake once and strain into a chilled champagne flute, garnish with a fresh slice of orange.

U-Boat

Like a German depth charge.
1-1/2 ounces Jagermeister in a shot glass
1/2 pint beer

Drop shot glass into beer glass and chug.

Hey Renee

Hey Renee

1/2 ounce Hana Bay 151 Rum
1/2 ounce Midori Melon Liqueur
1/2 ounce Amaretto
1 ounce Sweet and Sour

Shake and strain into a chilled 7-ounce martini glass, garnished with a fresh lemon wheel and bamboo orchid.

This one comes from Tod, one of my colleagues and a pillar of the Honolulu bartending community. I stopped by his place one night for an adult Pau Hana beverage and he sprung this on me. I liked it so much I had a couple of them. When I asked what he called it I swear I heard him say "Whisky Adobo" but it was kinda loud in the bar. Turns out he really wanted to name the drink "Whisky A-Go-Go" but I like what I heard better.

Whisky
Adobo

1 ounce Maker's Mark Bourbon
1/2 ounce Tuaca
Squeeze of 4 lemon wedges
1/2 tsp. sugar

Shake well. Serve in a chilled, sugar-rimmed martini glass, garnish with a lemon wheel and fresh mint sprig.

Whisky
Adobo

Dirty
Sanchez

My old pal Junior suggested the name and I made up a drink to go with it.

2 ounces Patron Silver Tequila
1/2 ounce Olive Juice

Shake once and strain into chilled martini glass, garnish with three large Spanish olives skewered on a green parasol.

Shooters

50

Okinawan
Pineapple

2 ounces Awamori Spirits CraZcrane Gold
2 ounces DeKuyper Tropical Pineapple Schnapps
Squeeze one fresh lime wedge

Shake once and strain into a chilled 7-ounce
martini glass, garnish with a fresh pineapple slice,
mint sprig, and green parasol.

*Yet another
instance of the
name coming before
I had created the
cocktail.*

Jagertini

2 ounces Absolut Citron Vodka
3/4 ounce Jagermeister
1/4 ounce Chambord
Juice from 1/4 lemon

Shake once and strain into a well-chilled
martini glass. Serve with a fresh lemon twist.

Bunda Lani

1 ounce Absolut Mandarin
1/2 ounce DeKuyper Tropical Pineapple
1/2 ounce Midori Melon Liqueur
1 ounce Cranberry Juice
Splash Sprite

Shake once and strain into a chilled
champagne flute, garnish with
a fresh slice of orange.

Z Tini

2 ounces Awamori Spirits CraZcrane
   Gold
1 ounce Zen Green Tea Liqueur
Squeeze two fresh lemon wedges

*Shake once and strain into a chilled
7-ounce martini glass, garnish
with a fresh lemon wheel.*

Shoot Z Root

1 ounce Awamori Spirits CraZcrane Gold
1/2 ounce Root Beer Schnapps
1/2 pint Beer

Drop shot glass into half pint of beer and chug.

Green Geisha

Green
Geisha

Randy and the gang at Awamori Spirits claim that the fermentation process makes CraZcrane so clean that you never get a hangover. Well, I'll be the judge of that.

2 ounces Awamori Spirits CraZcrane Gold
1 ounce Midori Melon Liqueur
Squeeze two fresh lime wedges

Shake once and strain into a chilled 7-ounce martini glass, garnish with a fresh lime wheel and sprig of mint.

Frozen
Drinks

*Just like the Tropical Cocktails,
most of these drinks will fill a
14-ounce hurricane-style glass.*

Waikoloan Sunset
Misty Rain
Mango Tango
Hi Boom Boom
Lava Lamp
Mango Mai Tai
It's All About Me
Mango Madness
Hawaiian Hillbilly
Green Mango
Annabelle's Midnight Snack

Waikoloan
Sunset

Waikoloan
Sunset

1-1/2 ounces Light Rum
1 ounce Mango Purée
3 ounces Strawberry Purée

Blend with crushed ice. Pour 1/2 ounce melted Vanilla Ice Cream into bottom of 14-ounce Hurricane glass. As you pour in the drink, the ice cream will swirl into the orange colored cocktail. Garnish with a fresh pineapple slice, bamboo orchid, and pink parasol.

Misty
Rain

Frank, an old regular of mine, sat at the bar and had dinner on a rainy night. He asked for something frozen, fruity, and refreshing to finish off his evening. I told him if he liked it he could name it and, after consuming about half his drink, he took out a pen and began scribbling on a beverage napkin. This is what he wrote: "Misty Rain. Born on a gloomy day over the Ko'olaus. A light mist of rain blesses our island, feeding the fruits that bring sunshine. The fruits of Hawai'i."

1 ounce 151 Proof Rum
3/4 ounce Peach Schnapps
3/4 ounce DeKuyper Tropical Pineapple
1 ounce Concentrated Sweet and Sour
1 ounce Strawberry Purée
2 ounces Mango Purée

Blend with crushed ice and serve in a 14-ounce Hurricane glass, garnish with a fresh pineapple slice, bamboo orchid, and a parasol.

Frozen Drinks

Mango Tango

1-1/2 ounces José Cuervo Gold Tequila
3/4 ounce Midori Melon Liqueur
1/4 ounce Rose's Lime Juice
3 ounces Mango Purée

Blend with crushed ice. Serve in a 14-ounce Hurricane glass, garnish with a fresh slice of mango, bamboo orchid, and a green parasol.

Hi Boom Boom

For reasons that I can't remember, Nohelani used to call me "Boom Boom."

1 ounce 151 Proof Rum
3/4 ounce Peach Schnapps
3 ounces Strawberry Purée

Blend with crushed ice. Pour into sugar-rimmed 14-ounce Hurricane glass, garnish with a fresh slice of a large strawberry, maraschino cherry, and a red parasol.

Frozen Drinks

Lava Lamp

Cuz it kinda looks like one…

1 ounce Mt. Gay Eclipse Rum
1/2 ounce Peach Schnapps
1/2 ounce Midori Melon Liqueur
3 ounces Concentrated Pineapple Juice

Blend with crushed ice. Pour 1/2 ounce melted Vanilla
Ice Cream and 1/2 ounce Strawberry Purée into Hurricane
glass then pour blended mixture into glass. Garnish with
a fresh lime wheel and a maraschino cherry.

Lava Lamp

Mango Mai Tai

Mango
Mai Tai

This is a fruit-flavored frozen version of a Hawaiian standard. You can substitute any other fruit purée for the mango—strawberry, and liliko'i (passion fruit) also work well.

1-1/2 ounces Light Rum
1/4 ounce Orange Curacao
1/4 ounce Orgeat Syrup
3 ounces Mango Purée
1-1/2 ounces Hana Bay Dark Rum

Blend first 4 ingredients with crushed ice. Float 1-1/2 ounces Hana Bay Dark Rum. Serve in a 14-ounce double old-fashioned glass, garnish with a fresh pineapple slice, mint sprig, and a maraschino cherry.

Frozen Drinks

It's All About Me

When you work in a resort in Hawai'i, you get to meet a few famous people from time to time. Most of the celebrities I've met were pretty cool, not wanting or expecting any special treatment, but there were one or two who thought that they owned the joint. There was this one actress, (we'll call her "Blank Blank") one of the stars in a fairly popular TV show back in the 70s, who asked me to make up a drink for her. When I did (and she loved it by the way) I told her she could name it, so she decided to call it the "Blank Blank" Special. Figures she'd name it after herself. Me, me, it's all about me.

3/4 ounce Bacardi Light Rum
1 ounce Midori Melon Liqueur
2 ounces Concentrated Liliko'i (passion fruit) Juice

Blend with crushed ice and serve in a 14-ounce double old-fashioned glass, garnish with a mint sprig and bamboo orchid.

Mango Madness

1 ounce Strawberry Purée
1 ounce Cruzan Mango Rum
3/4 ounce Peach Schnapps
Splash Rose's Lime Juice
3 ounces Mango Purée

Place Strawberry Purée in a 14-ounce Hurricane glass. Blend the remaining ingredients with crushed ice. Pour the mixture into the glass, on top of the strawberry purée. Garnish with a fresh mango slice, lime wheel, and mint sprig.

Frozen Drinks

Mango Madness

Hawaiian
Hillbilly

1 ounce Southern Comfort
1/2 ounce Captain Morgan Spiced Rum
3 ounces Guava Purée

Blend with crushed ice. Place 1 ounce melted Vanilla
Ice Cream into a 14-ounce Hurricane glass before
pouring in the mixture. Garnish with a fresh lime
wheel and 3 maraschino cherries.

*A few of
these and you'll
speak pidgin with a
Southern drawl.*

Hawaiian
Hillbilly

Green Mango

Green Mango

3/4 ounce Mt. Gay Eclipse Rum
3/4 ounce DeKuyper Sour Apple Pucker
3 ounces Mango Purée

Blend with crushed ice and serve in a 14-ounce Hurricane glass, garnish with a fresh slice of mango and bamboo orchid.

Annabelle always seemed to suggest this one to a customer at the end of the evening, right after I'd cleaned up and put away the blender.

Annabelle's Midnight Snack

1 ounce Blue Wave Raspberry Vodka
1 ounce DeKuyper Tropical Pineapple
1 ounce Mango Purée
2 ounces Raspberry Purée

Blend with crushed ice. Place 1 ounce melted Vanilla Ice Cream in the bottom of a 14-ounce Hurricane glass. As you pour the drink, the Ice Cream swirls into the orange colored cocktail. Garnish with a fresh pineapple slice, mint sprig, and parasol.

Frozen Drinks

Ice Cream
and
Dessert
Drinks

Cocoa Doodle Moo
My Pie
Mocha Monkey
M.I.A.
Elvis Has Left the Building
Chocolate Mambo
Chocolate Thunder
Chocolate Chip Cookie Dodo
Muddy Mud Pie
Chocolate Cake Shake
Cinnamon Apple Crumble Bumble
OREO Cookie Nookie
Macadamia Nut Job

Cocoa
Doodle Moo

1 ounce Captain Morgan Spiced Rum
1 ounce Dark Crème de Cacao
1/2 ounce Frangelico
2 ounces Half and Half

Shake ingredients and serve in a 14-ounce double old-fashioned glass, topped with whipped cream and a maraschino cherry.

My Pie

1 ounce Myers's Dark Rum
1 ounce Tuaca
3 ounces hot Apple Cider

Serve in a glass coffee mug and top with whipped cream and garnish with a cinnamon stick.

Mocha
Monkey

1 ounce Crème de Banana
1 ounce Dark Crème de Cacao
One whole peeled Banana
3 ounces Vanilla Ice Cream

*Blend ingredients and serve in a 14-ounce
Hurricane glass topped with whipped cream,
sliced banana, and shaved chocolate.*

M.I.A.

1 ounce Bailey's Irish Cream
1 ounce Kuya Fusion Rum
1/2 ounce Tia Maria
2 ounces Whole Milk

Shake ingredients and serve in a tall pint glass topped with whipped cream.

Elvis
Has Left
the Building

- 1/2 ounce 99 Bananas
- 1/2 ounce Frangelico
- 1/2 ounce Hana Bay 151 Proof Rum
- 2 ounces Vanilla Ice Cream
- 1 medium-sized banana
- 2 Reese's Peanut Butter Cups

Blend ingredients and serve in a tall pint glass, topped with whipped cream, sliced banana, and a Reese's Cup.

Chocolate
Mambo

1 ounce Light Rum
1/2 ounce Cointreau
1/2 ounce Dark Crème de Cacao
1 ounce Coconut Syrup
3 ounces Chocolate Ice Cream

Blend ingredients and serve in a 14-ounce Hurricane glass, topped with whipped cream and shredded coconut.

Chocolate
Thunder

1 ounce Dark Crème de Cacao
1 ounce Myers's Rum Cream
1 ounce Kahana Royale Macadamia Nut Liqueur
1 ounce Chocolate Syrup
3 ounces Vanilla Ice Cream

Swirl chocolate syrup in a 14-ounce Hurricane glass and pour in the mixture. Top with whipped cream, drizzle chocolate syrup on the whipped cream topping, and finally top with a maraschino cherry.

Chocolate
Thunder

And now for a little fun with desserts...
The following recipes will usually yield enough for two cocktails.
You'll have to let the blender run a while longer to liquefy
all the stuff in these concoctions, but believe me, it's worth the wait.

Chocolate Chip
Cookie Dodo

- 2 ounces Bacardi Vanilla Rum
- 3 ounces Tuaca
- 1 pint Ben and Jerry's Chocolate Chip Cookie Dough Ice Cream

Blend ingredients and serve in a 14-ounce Hurricane glass, topped with whipped cream and shaved chocolate.

Muddy Mud Pie

2 ounces Kahlua
3 ounces Whaler's Vanilla Rum
1 (8-ounce) Slice Mud Pie

Blend ingredients and serve in a 14-ounce double old-fashioned glass, topped with whipped cream and a few fresh coffee beans.

Chocolate Cake
Shake

- 2 ounces E&J Brandy Cream
- 2 ounces Tuaca
- 2 ounces Frangelico
- 1 (6-ounce) slice Chocolate Cake (the more layers and frosting the better)
- 2 ounces Vanilla Ice Cream

Blend ingredients and serve in a 14-ounce Hurricane glass, topped with whipped cream and shaved chocolate.

Chocolate Chip
Cookie Dodo

Oreo Cookie
Nookie

Cinnamon Apple
Crumble Bumble

2 ounces Dark Rum
2 ounces Goldschlager
2 ounces Grand Marnier
1 (6-ounce) slice Apple Pie, crust removed (or Apple Pie Filling right out of the can)
2 ounces Vanilla Ice Cream

Blend ingredients and serve in a 14-ounce Hurricane glass, topped with whipped cream, fresh apple slice, and powdered cinnamon.

Oreo Cookie
Nookie

2 ounces Captain Morgan's Spiced Rum
2 ounces Keoki Kona Coffee Liqueur
2 ounces Bailey's Irish Cream
8 ounces Vanilla Ice Cream
8 crushed Oreo Cookies

Put Oreo cookies in a small plastic bag and crush them with a liquor bottle or hard object until they're crushed up in little bitty pieces. Blend ingredients and serve in a 14-ounce hurricane glass, topped with whipped cream and an Oreo cookie.

Macadamia
Nut Job

Blend ingredients and serve in a 14-ounce Hurricane glass topped with whipped cream and chopped Macadamia nuts.

2 ounces Malibu Pineapple Rum
2 ounces Kahana Royale Macadamia Nut Liqueur
1 ounce B&B
1 (6-ounce) slice Macadamia Nut Pie, crust removed
2 ounces Vanilla Ice Cream

Classic
Gelatin
Party
Shots

A bunch of recipes for cocktails we all know and love that I've adapted for Gelatin.

57 T-Bird
Alabama Slammer
Apple Martini
Blazzing Saddles
Chocolate Martini
Creamsicle
Electric Iced Tea
Hairy Navel
Hawaiian Punch
Hurricane
Jolly Rancher
Kool Aid
Lemon Drop
Lifesaver
Long Island Iced Tea
Mai Tai
Margarita
Melon Ball
Nuclear Iced Tea
Pearl Harbor
Piña Colada
Pineapple Martini
Purple Hooter
Razztini
Red-Headed Slut
STP
Sex On The Beach
Sidecar
Singapore Sling
Strawberry
Margarita

Surfer on Acid
Toasted Almond
Tropical Itch
Woo Woo
Zombie

ORIGINAL RECIPE
GELATIN SHOTS
All Nuts
Almond Joy
B2 Stealth
Big Daddy
Big Island Iced Tea
Big Kahuna
Biohazard
Black Forest
Blue Meanie
Blue Surf
Brainless
Cherry Blossom
Cherry Bonbon
Chocolate Thunder
Don't Beam Me Up
Scotty (I'm Having
Too Much
Fun Here)
Five Alive
Georgia Peach
Grape Ape
Green M&M
Green Mango
Green Tea

Health Drink
Hiroshima
Hunky Monkey
Jamaican Me Crazy
Kamehameha
Kiwi Dream
Kohala Lighthouse
Koko's Melon
Adventure
Kool Aid
Maaaary
Mango Tango
Misty Rain
Mountain Doo Kine
Not Mom's Apple Pie
Nuclear Waste
Okinawan Pineapple
Paiea Punch
Peach Tea
Pineapple Breeze
Shipwreck
Sick Little Monkey
Southern Drawl
Tootsie Pop
Tuaca Drop
Waikoloan Sunset
Waimanalo Carnival
Ride
Whatamelon
Whisky Adobo
Windex

MAKING GELATIN SHOTS

Equipment you'll need:

One medium-sized saucepan for heating the water and melting the gelatin

One mixing spoon or whisk

A one-cup measuring cup

A four-cup or larger-size measuring cup for combining the melted gelatin mixture and the liquor, preferably with a pour spout for ease of pouring the mix into the shot cups

I prefer using 2-ounce plastic condiment cups with lids (usually available at any restaurant supply or wholesale club). The cups are shallow enough to allow you to run your tongue (or finger) around the edge and scrape the gelatin out. The lids make them easy to stack in the fridge and to transport in a cooler.

Directions:

Making gelatin shooters is pretty simple. Just follow the directions for making the gelatin provided on the box. Be sure to thoroughly melt the gelatin powder into the hot water and stir the mix constantly for two minutes. When the directions call for adding cold water to the melted gelatin mixture, substitute that same amount of whatever liquor(s) the shooter recipe calls for. Combine the melted gelatin mixture and the liquor(s) in the large (four-cup or larger) measuring cup.

Arrange the 2-ounce cups on a cookie sheet, pour the melted gelatin/liquor mixture into the cups, and slide the cookie sheet into your refrigerator. The set-up time in the refrigerator is longer than gelatin made without alcohol; most gelatin shooters will set in about 3 or 4 hours. The more potent the alcohol in the gelatin, the longer it will take to set. Allowing the gelatin to sit at least overnight works the best. A small (one cup) box of gelatin will yield fifteen 1-1/2-ounce gelatin shooters. When one of these recipes calls for two flavors of gelatin, melt both flavors together in two cups of hot water.

Tips:

Boil only the water, not the liquor. Boiling the liquor will only serve to cook off the alcohol, thus decreasing the potency of the gelatin shooters.

Do not use sugar-free gelatin. If you add alcohol to sugar-free gelatin, the gelatin will not set.

Do not try to add more than the specified amount of alcohol to make a more potent shot. If you use anything but a one to one ratio of hot water to alcohol, the gelatin will not set.

To get the gelatin shooters ready for transport to the party, I usually put all of the lidded shooters of each flavor into large (one gallon) zip lock plastic bags and pack them in a cooler full of ice.

Keep out of the reach of children. Kids love gelatin but this stuff isn't for them. If there will be children at the party, I usually make a few non-alcoholic shooters so they can have some too.

Most of these gelatin shooters taste like candy but they're very potent and can sneak up on you. Remember, each shooter, although small, is half alcohol. Be careful. Always enjoy liquor responsibly and never drink (in this case eat) and drive.

57 T-Bird

1/3 cup Vodka
1/3 cup Grand Marnier
1/3 cup Southern Comfort
Pineapple Gelatin

Alabama Slammer

1 cup Vodka
1 cup Southern Comfort
Orange and Apricot Gelatins

Apple Martini

3/4 cup Smirnoff Apple Twist
  Vodka
1/4 cup DeKuyper Sour Apple
  Pucker
Green Apple Gelatin

Blazing Saddles

1 cup Bourbon
1 cup Grand Marnier
Lemon and Orange Gelatins

Chocolate Martini

1/2 cup Light Crème de Cacao
1/2 cup Absolut Citron Vodka
Lemon Gelatin

Creamsicle

1 cup Absolut Citron Vodka
1/2 cup Triple Sec
1/2 cup Keoki Kona Coffee
    Liqueur
Orange and Lemon Gelatins

Electric Iced Tea

1/4 cup each Vodka, Gin, Light Rum, and Blue Curacao
Lemon Gelatin

Hairy Navel

1/2 cup Vodka
1/2 cup Peach Schnapps
Orange Gelatin

Hawaiian Punch

2/3 cup each Midori Melon Liqueur, Amaretto and Southern Comfort
Cranberry and Pineapple Gelatins

Hurricane

2/3 cup Light Rum
2/3 cup Dark Rum
2/3 cup Southern Comfort
Lemon and Cherry Gelatins

Jolly Rancher

1/2 cup Midori Melon Liqueur
1/2 cup Peach Schnapps
Lemon Gelatin

Kool Aid

1/5 cup each Vodka, Midori
  Melon Liqueur, Chambord,
  Amaretto, and Southern
  Comfort
Cran-Raspberry Gelatin

Lemon Drop

3/4 cup Absolut
   Citron Vodka
1/4 cup Triple Sec
Lemon Gelatin

Lifesaver

1/2 cup Malibu Coconut Rum
1/2 cup Butterscotch Schnapps
Pineapple Gelatin

Long Island Iced Tea

1/4 cup each Vodka, Gin,
   Triple Sec, and Hana Bay
   Dark Rum
Lemon Gelatin

Mai Tai

3/4 cup Light Rum
3/4 cup Dark Rum
1/4 cup Orange Curacao
1/4 cup Amaretto
Pineapple and Lemon Gelatins

Margarita

1-1/2 cups José cuervo Gold
   Tequila
1/2 cup Triple Sec
Lime and Orange Gelatins

Melon Ball

1/2 cup Vodka
1/2 cup Midori Melon Liqueur
Orange Gelatin

Nuclear Iced Tea

1/4 cup each Vodka, Gin, Light Rum, and Midori Melon Liqueur
Lemon Gelatin

Pearl Harbor

1/2 cup Midori Melon Liqueur
1/2 cup Light Rum
Pineapple Gelatin

Piña Colada

3/4 cup Malibu Coconut Rum
1/4 cup Hana Bay 151 Rum
Pineapple Gelatin

Pineapple Martini

3/4 cup Absolut Citron Vodka
1/4 cup DeKuyper Tropical
   Pineapple Schnapps
Pineapple Gelatin

Purple Hooter

2/3 cup Vodka
1/3 cup Chambord
Pineapple Gelatin

Razztini

3/4 cup Smirnoff Raspberry Twist
   Vodka
1/4 cup Chambord
Cran-Raspberry Gelatin

Red-Headed Slut

1/2 cup Jagermeister
1/2 cup Peach Schnapps
Cranberry Gelatin

STP

1/3 cup Malibu Coconut Rum
1/3 cup Midori Melon Liqueur
1/3 cup Blue Curacao
Pineapple Gelatin

Sex on the Beach

1 cup Vodka
1 cup Peach Schnapps
Orange and Cranberry
  Gelatins

Sidecar

2/3 cup Brandy
1/3 cup Grand Marnier
Lemon Gelatin

Singapore Sling

2/3 cup Sloe Gin
1-1/3 cup Cherry Brandy
Orange and Black Cherry
   Gelatins

Strawberry Margarita

3/4 cup José cuervo Gold Tequila
1/4 cup Triple Sec
Strawberry Gelatin

Surfer on Acid

1/3 cup Chambord (or any
   raspberry liqueur)
1/3 cup Jagermeister
1/3 cup Malibu Coconut Rum
Pineapple Gelatin

Toasted Almond

1/2 cup Kahlua
1/2 cup Amaretto
Lemon Gelatin

Tropical Itch

1/2 cup Hana Bay Dark Rum
1/2 cup Hana Bay 151 Rum
1/2 cup Orange Curacao
1/2 cup Bourbon
Pineapple and Lemon
   Gelatins

Woo Woo

2/3 cup Absolut Peach Vodka
1/3 cup Peach Schnapps
Cranberry Gelatin

Zombie

1/2 cup Hana Bay Dark Rum
1/2 cup Hana Bay 151 Rum
1/2 cup Orange Curacao
1/2 cup Amaretto
Pineapple and Orange Gelatins

ORIGINAL RECIPE GELATIN SHOTS

Almond Joy

1/2 cup Amaretto
1/4 cup Malibu Coconut
  Rum
1/4 cup Light Crème de
  Cacao
Lemon Gelatin

All Nuts

1/2 cup Hana Bay 151 Rum
1/2 cup Amaretto
1/2 cup Frangelico
1/2 cup Kahana Royale
  Macadamia Nut Liqueur
Lemon and Peach Gelatins

B2 Stealth

1/2 cup Hana Bay 151 Rum
1/2 cup Peach Schnapps
Pineapple Gelatin

Big Daddy

2 cups Myers's Dark Rum
Cranberry and Lemon Gelatins

Big Island Iced Tea

1/4 cup each Vodka, Gin, Hana
Bay Dark Rum, and DeKuyper
Tropical Pineapple Schnapps
Lemon Gelatin

Big Kahuna

1 cup Hana Bay 151 Rum
1 cup DeKuyper Tropical
Pineapple Schnapps
Pineapple and Orange Gelatins

Biohazard

1/2 cup Hana Bay 151 Rum
1/2 cup Jagermeister
1 cup DeKuyper Strawberry
    Schnapps
Pineapple and Wild Strawberry
    Gelatins

Black Forest

1/2 cup Bacardi Coco
    Rum
1/2 cup Vandermint
    Chocolate Mint
    Liqueur
Black Cherry Gelatin

Blue Meanie

1/2 cup DeKuyper Island Blue
    Pucker
1/2 cup Absolut Citron Vodka
Berry Blue Gelatin

Blue Surf

1/2 cup Kuya Fusion Rum
1/2 cup DeKuyper Island Blue
    Pucker
Berry Blue Gelatin

Brainless

1 cup Kuya Fusion Rum
1 cup Tuaca
Pineapple and Lemon
    Gelatins

Cherry Blossom

3/4 cup Awamori Spirits
    CraZcrane Silver
1/4 cup Tuaca
Cherry Gelatin

Cherry Bonbon

1/3 cup Smirnoff Citrus Twist
   Vodka
2/3 cup Light Crème de Cacao
Cherry Gelatin

Chocolate Thunder

1/3 cup Light Crème de Cacao
1/3 cup Bacardi Coco Rum
1/3 cup Kahana Royale
   Macadamia Nut Liqueur
Lemon Gelatin

Don't Beam Me Up Scotty

(I'm Having Too Much Fun Here)

1/4 cup DeKuyper Tropical Pineapple
   Schnapps
1/2 cup Absolut Citron Vodka
Strawberry-Kiwi Gelatin

Five Alive

1/5 cup each Absolut Raspberry,
   Absolut Vanilla, Absolut
   Apeach, Absolut Mandarin, and
   Absolut Citron Vodkas
Orange Gelatin

Georgia Peach

3/4 cup Absolut Apeach Vodka
1/4 cup Peach Schnapps
Peach Gelatin

Grape Ape

1/2 cup Smirnoff Apple Twist
   Vodka
1/2 cup Midori Melon Liqueur
Grape Gelatin

Green M&M

2/3 cup Frangelico
1/3 cup Light Crème de Cacao
Green Apple Gelatin

Green Mango

1/2 cup Hana Bay Gold Rum
1/2 cup DeKuyper Sour Apple
   Pucker
Mango Gelatin

Green Tea

2/3 cup Awamori Spirits CraZcrane
   Gold
1/3 cup Zen Green Tea Liqueur
Lemon Gelatin

Health Drink

4 cups Absolut Citron Vodka
Pineapple, Orange,
  Strawberry, and Lemon
  Gelatins

Hiroshima

1/2 cup Midori Melon Liqueur
1/2 cup Peach Schnapps
1 cup Hana Bay 151 Rum
Apricot and Pineapple Gelatins

Hunky Monkey

1/2 cup 99 Bananas
1/2 cup Light Crème de Cacao
Strawberry-Banana Gelatin

Jamaican Me Crazy

1/4 cup each Myers's Dark Rum, Malibu Coconut Rum, Captain Morgan Spiced Rum, and Blue Curacao
Pineapple Gelatin

Kamehameha

1 cup Okolehao Liqueur
1 cup DeKuyper Tropical Pineapple Schnapps
Pineapple and Mango Gelatins

Kiwi Dream

1/2 cup Smirnoff Strawberry Twist Vodka
1/2 cup Bols Kiwi Liqueur
Strawberry-Kiwi Gelatin

Kohala Lighthouse

1/2 cup Stolichnaya Vodka
1/2 cup Grand Marnier
Lime Gelatin

Koko's Melon Adventure

1-1/3 cups Vodka
2/3 cup Midori Melon
  Liquer
Pineapple and Lemon
  Gelatins

Kool Aid

1/5 cup each Vodka, Midori
  Melon Liqueur, Chambord,
  Amaretto, and Southern
  Comfort
Cran-Raspberry Gelatin

Maaaary

1/2 cup Stoly Strawberry Vodka
1/2 cup DeKuyper Sour Apple
  Pucker
Cranberry Gelatin

Mango Tango

1/2 Cup José Cuervo Gold
  Tequila
1/2 cup Midori Melon Liqueur
Mango Gelatin

Misty Rain

2/3 cup Hana Bay 151 Rum
2/3 cup Peach Schnapps
2/3 cup DeKuyper Tropical
  Pineapple Schnapps
Strawberry and Mango Gelatins

Mountain Doo Kine

(Three-cup recipe)

1 cup Absolut Mandarin Vodka
1 cup Absolut Citron Vodka
1 cup Midori Melon Liqueur
Lemon, Lime, and Orange
  Gelatins

Not Mom's Apple Pie

1/2 cup Aftershock Cinnamon
  Schnapps
1/2 cup Smirnoff Green Apple
  Twist Vodka
Green Apple Gelatin

Nuclear Waste

1/2 cup Hana Bay 151 Rum
1/2 cup Midori Melon Liqueur
Apricot Gelatin

Okinawan Pineapple

1/2 cup Awamori Spirits
   CraZcrane Silver
1/2 cup DeKuyper Tropical
   Pineapple Schnapps
Pineapple Gelatin

Pai'ea Punch

1/3 cup Myers's Dark Rum
2/3 cup DeKuyper Tropical
   Pineapple Schnapps
Cranberry Gelatin

Peach Tea

2/3 cup Awamori Spirits
   CraZcrane Silver
1/3 cup Zen Green Tea Liqueur
Peach Gelatin

Pineapple Breeze

3/4 cup Malibu Pineapple Rum
1/4 cup Kahana Royale
    Macadamia Nut Liqueur
Pineapple Gelatin

Shipwreck

1/2 cup 99 Bananas
1/2 cup Malibu Coconut Rum
Pineapple Gelatin

Sick Little Monkey

1/2 cup 99 Bananas
1/2 cup DeKuyper Strawberry
    Schnapps
Strawberry-Banana Gelatin

Southern Drawl

1/2 cup Jack Daniels
1/2 cup Southern Comfort
Peach Gelatin

Tootsie Pop

1/2 cup Absolut Citron Vodka
1/4 cup Kahlua
1/4 cup Dark Creme de Cacao
Lemon Gelatin

Tuaca Drop

1/2 cup Absolut Citron Vodka
1/2 cup Tuaca
Lemon Gelatin

Waikoloan Sunset

1 cup Bacardi Limon Rum
1 cup Hana Bay 151 Rum
Mango and Strawberry Gelatins

Waimānalo Carnival Ride

1 cup Absolut Mandarin Vodka
1/2 cup Stoly Raspberry Vodka
1/2 cup DeKuyper Sour Apple Pucker
Cranberry and Lemon Gelatins

Whatamelon

1/2 cup Smirnoff Watermelon
   Twist Vodka
1/2 cup Midori Melon Liqueur
Watermelon Gelatin

Whisky Adobo

2/3 cup Maker's Mark Bourbon
1/3 cup Tuaca
Lemon Gelatin

Windex

2/3 cup Blue Wave Raspberry
   Vodka
1/3 cup Blue Curacao
Lemon Gelatin

Index

ginger ale, 22, 23, 42
glass
  double old-fashioned, 10, 23, 26,
    65, 66, 74, 80
  Hurricane, ix, 5, 8, 11, 14, 15, 20, 21,
    22, 23, 25, 28, 59, 60, 61, 62,
    68, 71, 75, 77, 78, 80, 83,
    85, 93
  martini, 1, 37, 38, 39, 40, 42, 43,
    47, 48, 50, 51, 53, 55
  old-fashioned, 10, 23, 26, 36, 37,
    38, 39, 44, 65, 66, 74, 80
  rocks, 5, 36
Goldschlager, 83
Grand Marnier, 13, 35, 83, 90, 91, 99,
  112
Grenadine, 14, 36
guava purée, 68

H

Half and Half, 37
horseradish 31

I

Ice Cream, viii, 59, 62, 67, 68, 72, 74,
  75, 76, 77, 78, 80, 81, 82, 83

J

Jack Daniels, 117
Jagermeister, 45, 51, 98, 100, 105
jigger, 3
juice
  cranberry, 10, 13, 14, 19, 20, 21,
    23, 38, 40, 42, 43, 45, 52
  fruit, 2
  lemon, 31
  liliko'i, 11, 20, 38, 66
  lime, 8
  olive, 50
  orange, 10, 14, 22, 23, 27, 36,
    45
  pineapple, 8, 10, 13, 14, 15, 22, 23,
    39, 42, 45, 62
  Rose's Lime Juice, 35, 61, 71
  tomato juice, 31

K

Kahana Royale Macadamia Nut Liqueur,

15, 36, 78, 83, 103, 107, 116
Kahlua, 15, 22, 39, 80, 100, 117
Keoki Kona Coffee Liqueur, 36, 83, 91

L

lemonade concentrate, 27

M

macadamia nut pie, 83
Maker's Mark Bourbon, 48, 119
mango purée, 21, 59, 60, 61, 65, 66
martini, 1, 37, 38, 39, 40, 42, 43, 47,
  48, 50, 51, 53, 55
Midori Melon Liqueur, 8, 13, 27, 44, 45,
  47, 52, 55, 61, 62, 66, 92, 93, 95, 96,
  98, 108, 110, 112, 113, 114, 119
milk, 76
Miller Lite Beer, 27
muddler, 4
Mud Pie, viii, 73, 80
Myers's Rum Cream, 78

O

Okolehao Liqueur, 111
Orange Curacao, 10, 14, 65, 95, 100,
  101
Orgeat Syrup, 10, 65

P

pepper, 31
pint, 10, 14, 16, 19, 27, 31, 42, 45, 53,
  76, 80
pour spout, 4, 87

R

Red Bull, 44
Reese's Peanut Butter Cups, 76
Rose's Lime Juice, 35, 61, 66
rum, 36
  151 Proof, 13, 20, 39, 43, 60, 61, 76
  Bacardi
    Coco, 105, 107
    Light, 66
    Limon, 38, 118
    Razz, 25
    Vanilla, 80
  Captain Morgan Spiced, 68, 74,
    111

Index